Tammy Duckworth

Published in the United States of America by Cherry Lake Publishing
Ann Arbor, Michigan
www.cherrylakepublishing.com

Reading Adviser: Marla Conn, MS, Ed, Literacy specialist, Read-Ability, Inc.
Book Designer: Jennifer Wahi
Illustrator: Jeff Bane

Photo Credits: ©Alex Pix/Shutterstock, 5; ©Doucefleur/Shutterstock, 7; ©Have a nice day Photo/Shutterstock, 9; ©Karolis Kavolelis/Shutterstock, 11; ©Rudi Williams/U.S. Department of Defense/Public Domain, 13, 22; ©Gregory Reed/Shutterstock, 15; ©Kelly Bell/Shutterstock, 17; ©Department of Veterans Affairs/U.S. Department of Defense/Public Domain, 19; ©United States Congress/Wikimedia/Public Domain, 21, 23; Jeff Bane, cover, 1, 8, 12, 16

The appearance of U.S. Department of Defense (DoD) visual information does not imply or constitute DoD endorsement of Defense.

Library of Congress Cataloging-in-Publication Data

Names: Sarantou, Katlin, author. | Bane, Jeff, 1957- illustrator.
Title: Tammy Duckworth / by Katlin Sarantou ; illustrated by Jeff Bane.
Description: Ann Arbor, MI : Cherry Lake Publishing, [2019] | Series: My
   itty-bitty bio | Includes bibliographical references and index. |
   Audience: Grades K-3.
Identifiers: LCCN 2019004204| ISBN 9781534147041 (hardcover) | ISBN
   9781534148475 (pdf) | ISBN 9781534149908 (pbk.) | ISBN 9781534151338
   (hosted ebook)
Subjects: LCSH: Duckworth, Tammy, 1968---Juvenile literature. | Women
   legislators--United States--Biography--Juvenile literature. |
   Legislators--United States--Biography--Juvenile literature. | United
   States. Congress. Senate--Biography--Juvenile literature. | Women
   politicians--United States--Biography--Juvenile literature. | Thai
   Americans--Illinois--Chicago--Biography--Juvenile literature. | Illinois.
   General Assembly. House of Representatives--Biography--Juvenile literature.
Classification: LCC E840.8.D83 S27 2019 | DDC 328.73/092 [B] --dc23
LC record available at https://lccn.loc.gov/2019004204

Printed in the United States of America
Corporate Graphics

About the author: Katlin Sarantou grew up in the cornfields of Ohio. She enjoys reading and dreaming of faraway places.

About the illustrator: Jeff Bane and his two business partners own a studio along the American River in Folsom, California, home of the 1849 Gold Rush. When Jeff's not sketching or illustrating for clients, he's either swimming or kayaking in the river to relax.

I was born in Thailand in 1968.

My family moved a lot. We settled in Hawaii. I was 16.

Where would you like to live?

Times were tough. We had to use **food stamps**.

I took jobs to help out.

How have you helped your parents?

I went to college. I studied **political science**.

I joined the army. There weren't many positions open to women.

I chose to fly helicopters.

I was sent to Iraq.

My helicopter was attacked.

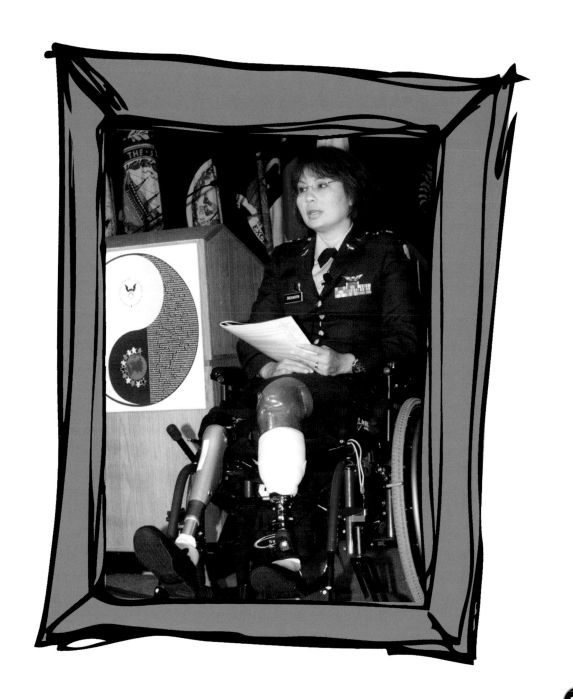

I lost my legs.

But I didn't let it stop me.

What problem has been difficult for you?

I received a **purple heart**.

I became a public supporter for **veterans**.

I served two **terms** in the **House of Representatives**. I represented Illinois.

I am the first woman from Thailand in the U.S. **Congress**.

I currently work in the government.

I continue to help women and veterans.

Everyone should be treated fairly.

What would you like to ask me?

2004

1960

Born
1968

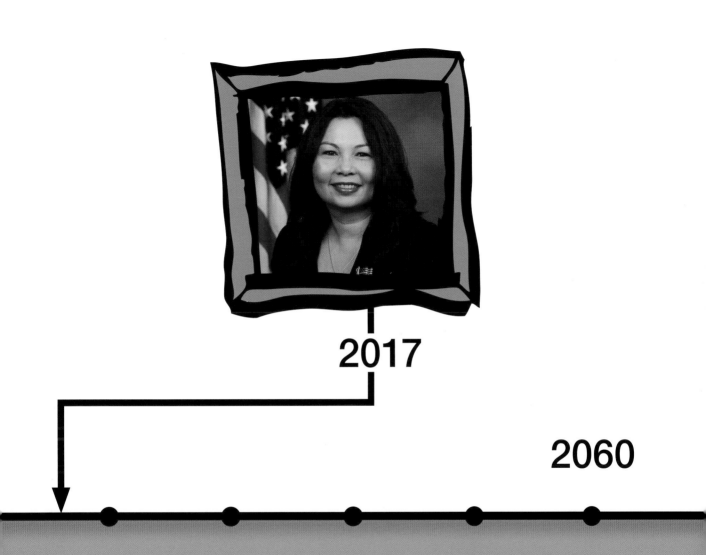

2017

2060

glossary

Congress (KAHNG-gris) the lawmaking part of the U.S. government, made up of the House of Representatives and the Senate

food stamps (FOOD STAMPS) a government program that helps poor people buy food

House of Representatives (HOUS UHV rep-rih-ZEN-tuh-tivz) a part of the U.S. Congress that works to make laws

political science (puh-LIT-ih-kuhl SYE-uhns) the study of government systems

purple heart (PUR-puhl HART) a military medal for those wounded or killed in battle

terms (TURMZ) periods of time when a person holds an official office

veterans (VET-ur-uhnz) former members of the armed forces

index